D1518824

A Celebration of the Civil Rights Movement ™

AFFIRMATIVE ACTION: LEGISLATING EQUALITY AND OPPORTUNITY

Mary-Lane Kamberg

ROSEN
PUBLISHING®

New York

For Amy Ladewig Phillips

Published in 2015 by The Rosen Publishing Group, Inc.
29 East 21st Street, New York, NY 10010

Copyright © 2015 by The Rosen Publishing Group, Inc.

First Edition

All rights reserved. No part of this book may be reproduced in any form without permission in writing from the publisher, except by a reviewer.

Library of Congress Cataloging-in-Publication Data

Kamberg, Mary-Lane.
Affirmative action: legislating equality and opportunity/by Mary-Lane Kamberg.
p. cm.—(A celebration of the Civil Rights Movement)
Includes index.
ISBN 978-1-4777-7741-1 (library binding)
1. Affirmative action programs—United States—Juvenile literature.
2. Discrimination in employment—United States—History—Juvenile literature. 3. Discrimination in education—United States—History—Juvenile literature. I. Kamberg, Mary-Lane, 1948-. II. Title.
HF5549.5.A34 K36 2015
331.13—d23

Manufactured in the United States of America

CONTENTS

which shall be determined by adding to the whole Number of
taxed, three fifths of all other Persons. The actual Enumeration

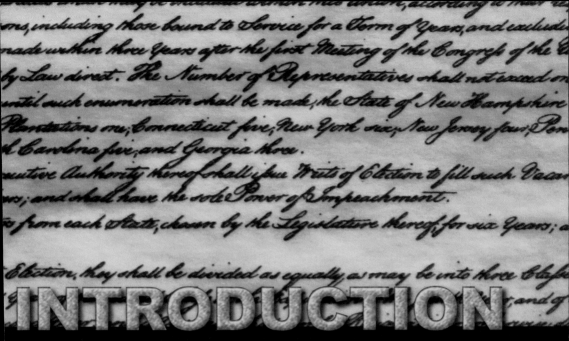

INTRODUCTION

Until the mid-1960s, America's classrooms and offices looked quite different from today's. Classrooms were separated according to race. In the workforce, white men held nearly all management positions. Women worked as secretaries. People of color worked as janitors.

It took fifty years and actions by U.S. presidents, Congress, the Supreme Court, and voters in statewide elections to come up with the laws and regulations for schools and workplaces in effect today. President John F. Kennedy was the first U.S. president to take steps to give people of color more opportunities. He signed an executive order that required businesses fulfilling contracts with the federal government to take "affirmative action" to ensure lack of racial bias in employment.

President John F. Kennedy spearheaded congressional action on the Civil Rights Act, which was signed into law by President Lyndon B. Johnson in 1964 after Kennedy's death.

Affirmative action refers to a plan, program, or policy that makes an active effort to improve the employment or educational opportunities for minorities and women. President Lyndon B. Johnson further defined the term. He wanted to see "equality as a fact and equality as a result." He wanted African Americans to have the same chances as whites to learn, grow, work, share in society, and pursue individual happiness. And he wanted schools and businesses to take steps to make it happen.

It was not enough to wait until a minority applicant arrived. Johnson expected active recruiting of minorities—and later, women—in hiring and college admissions. As affirmative action plans went into effect, however, the equal opportunity rights of minorities seemed to collide with the rights of others. Would minority hiring mean unfair treatment of whites? Would qualified white applicants be denied admission to institutions of higher learning in favor of less qualified minority students?

Lawsuits made their way to the district courts, courts of appeal, and eventually the U.S. Supreme Court. Judicial decisions further shaped and limited what affirmative action policies could and could not include. Early verdicts favored the use of affirmative action plans. However, as more cases were heard, courts limited their application.

Meanwhile, organizations opposed affirmative action on the grounds that preferences in favor of some violated the equal protection of all under the Fourteenth Amendment to the U.S. Constitution. The amendment reads, in part, "No state shall make or enforce any law which shall abridge the privileges or immunities of citizens of the United States…nor deny to any person within its jurisdiction the equal protection of the laws." Voters in eighteen states approved new laws or amendments to their state constitutions that banned affirmative action in schools and businesses.

Affirmative action began as a temporary measure to right the wrongs of the past that kept minorities at a disadvantage in nearly all areas of life. Some believe affirmative action will no longer be necessary in the future. Others, however, fear that America may never be free from discrimination without it.

Chapter 1

A LEVEL PLAYING FIELD

WHITE WAITING ROOM *and* RESTAURANT

Before the Civil Rights Act passed, whites and people of color led separate lives. Segregation kept people from interacting in areas of public accommodation.

When the Civil War ended, three amendments to the U.S. Constitution ended slavery, gave citizenship to former slaves, and gave voting rights to all men no matter their race. However, many white citizens in the defeated South refused to accept the changes. State governments imposed taxes and used literacy tests to keep African Americans from voting. Other state and local "Jim Crow" laws, first passed in the 1880s, kept minorities out of whites-only classrooms, restrooms, theaters, and railroad cars. The laws separated the races and allowed favoritism toward whites in all walks of life.

WHO WAS JIM CROW?

After the Reconstruction era, white Southerners followed so-called Black Codes, which were rules, customs, and laws that upheld segregation and denied rights that the Thirteenth, Fourteenth, and Fifteenth Amendments to the U.S. Constitution had granted to blacks. The laws included in the Black Codes became known as Jim Crow laws.

Jim Crow was a song-and-dance "grinning fool" character in minstrel shows in the nineteenth century and later in vaudeville performances. Jim Crow was first played in 1828 by Thomas Dartmouth "Daddy" Rice. The white actor wore blackface theatrical makeup that used a layer of burnt cork over a layer of cocoa butter and red or white makeup that exaggerated lips, similar to a circus clown's. The character created stereotypes of a "happy-go-lucky plantation darky" and a "dandified coon."

Other white entertainers adopted the character in performances throughout the United States and Europe. Such other blackface characters as Mammy, Buck, and Zip Coon populated acts that included imitations of black singing and dancing, along with jokes and skits performed using a "plantation" dialect.

Well before the Civil War, the term "Jim Crow" was in common use as a racial slur for blacks. However, by the beginning of the twentieth century, the term ceased use as a racial epithet, instead referring to antiblack laws and customs.

An 1896 Supreme Court ruling, *Plessy v. Ferguson*, supported the idea of "separate but equal" facilities, which let governments segregate the white and black races as long as both got the same treatment. The fact was, however, that in

Although the U.S. Supreme Court approved the use of "separate but equal" schools, in practice the ones open to minority students most often offered a substandard education.

practice the "facilities" were far from equal. Failing schools in minority neighborhoods graduated students who were ill-prepared to compete with whites from better schools. Businesses set employment requirements that few minority applicants could meet.

Discriminatory practices continued into the twentieth century. In 1954, the Supreme Court reversed itself in *Brown v. Board of Education of Topeka* (Kansas), declaring racial bias in education unconstitutional. Forced school integration followed. Districts bused students from black or white neighborhoods to schools in each other's areas. Civil rights activists staged sit-ins and other peaceful protests to call attention to the oppression African Americans faced. The issue was not going away.

In 1957, Congress established a civil rights section of the Justice Department. It also set up a Commission on Civil Rights, which investigated reported cases of discrimination. Congress later tried to help blacks register to vote through court-appointed referees. These attempts did little to address the other main complaints of civil rights leaders: unfair practices in employment and education.

MAKE IT HAPPEN

After nearly a decade of racial unrest, President John F. Kennedy took steps to address unfair employment practices that, at best, favored whites and, at worst, prevented minorities from getting jobs at all. Kennedy envisioned a temporary solution—one that would stay in effect only until all Americans competed for jobs on a level playing field.

On March 6, 1961, Kennedy cited an "urgent need" to promote full equality of employment opportunity. He issued Executive Order 10925, where he noted that discrimination based on race, creed, color, or national origin is unconstitutional. The executive order created the President's Committee on Equal Employment Opportunity to study and keep track of hiring practices by government departments and agencies, as well as businesses seeking to provide goods and services to the federal government. The executive order allowed the committee to recommend additional steps needed to support the policy.

One such step was the requirement that all help-wanted notices include a statement of equal opportunity. Further, government contractors had to take "affirmative action" to ensure that applicants and employees were treated the same without regard to their race, creed, color, or national origin.

A MORAL ISSUE

Kennedy also proposed new legislation. In a televised address to the nation on June 11, 1963, he said, "We are confronted primarily with a moral issue...The heart of the question is whether all Americans are afforded equal rights and equal opportunities...One hundred years of delay have passed since President Abraham Lincoln freed the slaves, yet their heirs, their grandsons, are not fully free. They are not yet free from the bonds of injustice. And this nation, for all its hopes and all its boasts, will not be fully free until all of its citizens are free."

A week later, Kennedy sent his proposed civil rights legislation to Congress. Five months later, however, the president was dead. His vice president, Lyndon B. Johnson, replaced him and pushed for passage of Kennedy's bill, which southern Democrats in the senate strongly opposed.

PASSAGE AND ENFORCEMENT

The Civil Rights Act was passed in 1964, and President Johnson signed it into law on July 2 of that year. The law was

WOMEN UNDER THE WIRE

A congressman who opposed the Civil Rights Act in general wound up ensuring that women be included as a protected class under the proposed law. Howard W. Smith was a Democrat from Virginia who chaired the House Rules Committee. Days before Congress was set to vote on the Civil Rights Act, Smith proposed adding the term "sex" to Title VII of the act, which lists all the ways Americans cannot be discriminated against when it comes to employment.

Several of Smith's fellow Democrats opposed gender equality in the workplace largely because labor unions didn't want women in their ranks. Some historians think Smith proposed the amendment hoping that it would help defeat the bill. In fact, the congressional record indicates that congressmen laughed out loud when Smith proposed his amendment. However, Smith said he wasn't joking. He believed in equal rights for women—if not for minorities.

fairly wide sweeping, covering employment, education, and voting rights. It banned segregation based on race, gender, religion, or national origin in all places of public lodging and with regard to housing. It also outlawed discrimination by employers and labor unions.

After passage of the act, the Equal Employment Opportunity Commission (EEOC) was created with the power to sue whoever violated the law about hiring and firing practices. Franklin D. Roosevelt Jr. was the commission's first chair. Roosevelt wanted to encourage businesses to be

President Lyndon B. Johnson shakes hands with civil rights leader Dr. Martin Luther King Jr. after signing the Civil Rights Act into law on July 2, 1964.

even more aggressive in recruiting and training than the law required. He vowed not only to investigate complaints of job discrimination, but also to use affirmative action to correct violations.

The Civil Rights Act authorized the federal Office of Education to promote school desegregation. The law also prohibited discrimination with regard to voting requirements. A year later, the Voting Rights Act of 1965 outlawed literacy tests for voters.

BY THE NUMBERS

A year after signing the Civil Rights Act, President Johnson spoke at graduation ceremonies at Howard University, a historically black university in Washington, D.C. Using the term of the times, he cited examples of conditions experienced by "Negro Americans," including:

- In 1930, the unemployment rates for blacks and whites were roughly equal; in 1965, the rate for African Americans was twice that of whites.
- In 1948, the unemployment rate for African American teenage boys was 8 percent—lower than that of whites. By 1964, the African American rate was 23 percent, while that for whites was 13 percent.
- Between 1955 and 1957, the unemployment rate for experienced African Americans was 22 percent. Between 1961 and 1963, the rate was 29 percent.
- White families living in poverty had decreased 27 percent since the end of World War II. But nonwhite families living in poverty decreased only 3 percent.
- In 1940, nonwhite infant mortality was 70 percent higher than for whites. By 1962, the gap had widened to 90 percent higher.

DEFINING AFFIRMATIVE ACTION

Johnson knew that the new laws only began to end discrimination. The president added that African Americans were increasingly isolated from white communities as people of

Attendees of the 1965 graduation ceremony at Howard University in Washington, D.C., react to President Johnson addressing the meaning of equality during his commencement speech.

color moved into the urban core and became a "city within a city."

"The harsh fact of the matter is that in the battle for true equality, too many—far too many—are losing ground every day," Johnson said in a speech at Howard University, a historically black university in Washington D.C.

He said, "Freedom is the right to share, share fully and equally, in American society—to vote, to hold a job, to enter a public place, to go to school. It is the right to be treated in every part of our national life as a person equal in dignity and promise to all others."

He added that freedom was not enough. A true remedy went beyond "equality as a right and a theory." He wanted to see "equality as a fact and equality as a result." Historians point to the Howard University speech as Johnson's definition of affirmative action.

Chapter 2

NEW ATTITUDES

Changing people's attitudes and behaviors would take more than a president's signature on a piece of paper. Backlash from southern Democrats began almost at once. They argued that the Civil Rights Act hurt American values of self-reliance and gave a free ride to unqualified or underqualified workers. They said opening doors for minorities meant closing doors for whites, what some called "reverse discrimination."

Senators Everett McKinley Dirksen and Hubert Humphrey *(seated, left to right)* celebrate the vote that stopped debate and allowed voting on the 1964 Civil Rights Act.

Senator Everett Dirksen, who helped write the law, argued that it did not require employers to give anyone special treatment. Republicans and northern Democrats celebrated the Civil Rights Act as a way to make the "land of opportunity" apply to people who came to America as slaves, as well as future generations to come.

CHANGES AFOOT

Despite the new law, discrimination in housing, employment, and education continued. In the workplace, whites still held higher positions and earned higher pay. So President Johnson took further steps to encourage change. He asked Vice President Hubert Humphrey to review federal agencies' activities concerning civil rights.

Humphrey based his recommendations on the idea that, whenever possible, affirmative action plans should be performed by departments and agencies as distinguished from interagency committees.

Under President Kennedy's order to federal employers and contractors, the President's Committee on Equal Employment Opportunity had oversight responsibilities. Secretary of Labor W. Willard Wirtz, who served as vice chair of the committee, was responsible for reviewing complaints and coordinating the efforts of various federal departments and agencies to make sure that nondiscrimination requirements for government contractors were followed. With the formation of the Equal Employment Opportunity Commission after passage of the Civil Rights Act, Humphrey recommended an upgrade to the secretary's authority. In a

HINTON SHOCKLEY'S STORY

Hinton Shockley is an African American who spent four years in the U.S. Air Force learning the trade of aircraft structural technician. In short, he was an aircraft mechanic. He left the service in 1963 and applied for a mechanic's job at Trans World Airlines (TWA) in Kansas City, Missouri.

"They told me they didn't hire minorities as mechanics," Shockley said. "They offered me a job as a janitor."

Instead, in January 1964, Shockley took a job as a spot welder at the Ford Motor Company's Kansas City assembly plant in nearby Claycomo, Missouri. In 1966, a coworker on the assembly line told him TWA was hiring and suggested he apply again. However, the suggestion came with a warning: "If you don't know anyone there, you probably won't get hired."

Upon hearing that, Shockley made a personal phone call to the aircraft structural manager to request an interview. Based on Shockley's qualifications, the manager granted him a formal interview. Shockley got the job. He worked at TWA for thirty-three years and retired in 1999.

"The times changed, and the company changed," Shockley said. "I'm glad I was there when they did."

memo to the president, Humphrey wrote that "responsibility should now be vested directly in the Department of Labor, and I so recommend."

In keeping with his vision for the United States, Johnson issued Executive Order 11246 on September 24, 1965. The order built on language included in Kennedy's 1961 executive order. Where Kennedy had told federal employers and contractors to avoid employment discrimination, Johnson gave the order teeth. He gave the secretary of labor enforcement authority to ensure that covered employers take "affirmative action" to offer minorities equal opportunities. Wirtz established the Office of Federal Contract Compliance (OFCC), with Edward C. Sylvester Jr. as its first director.

In 1966, the newly formed National Organization for Women (NOW) demanded that the EEOC carry out its legal mandate to end sex discrimination in employment. NOW didn't like that the EEOC let companies run employment ads in newspapers that separated genders: "Help Wanted Male"

NAACP executive director Roy Wilkins *(center right)* speaks with Dr. King in 1967. A year earlier, Wilkins had urged employment equality at a White House conference.

and "Help Wanted Female." In 1967, President Johnson amended Executive Order 11246 to end unfair practices on the basis of gender.

Also in 1966, Roy Wilkins, executive director of the National Association for the Advancement of Colored People (NAACP), urged that strong measures were required to ease African American unemployment. Speaking at a White House civil rights conference, he said, "Negro unemployment is of disaster proportions. Creative and large-scale action must be taken to achieve full and fair employment for the Negro working-age population."

ENFORCEMENT IN ACTION

Both the EEOC and the OFCC were underfunded and under-staffed. According to the book *Historical Guides to Controversial Issues in America: Affirmative Action,* the EEOC had enough money and personnel to handle only two thousand of the nine thousand complaints it received in its first year. Unable to deal individually with everything that came their way, the EEOC and OFCC decided to work together, focusing their efforts on major contractors and industries that got the biggest federal contracts.

The EEOC had received several complaints about the Newport News Shipbuilding and Drydock Company, a major defense contractor in Newport News, Virginia. The agency investigated complaints that black workers got lower pay than whites for the same work and that blacks were not allowed access to apprenticeship programs or promotions. There were also clear signs that some jobs were filled only by white workers. The possibility that the company could lose fed-eral contracts, as well as face a lawsuit, encouraged company

SLOW PROGRESS

Although the federal agencies charged with enforcing affirmative action policies had some success, by 1967, employment statistics showed little change. Most companies in America had no official policies against hiring or promoting blacks or women. More concerning, some business practices still kept blacks and women from getting jobs or promotions; education requirements, seniority, and promotion tests frequently left minorities behind. The EEOC's policies of aggressive recruiting and training of minorities clearly had not worked as well as hoped.

officials to change their ways. The EEOC came to an agreement with the company that called for equal pay for equal work, regardless of race. Many black employees were given promotions, and the company was required to open up apprenticeship programs to everyone.

After learning that many southern textile mills employed only white workers, the EEOC encouraged African Americans to seek jobs in the industry. The OFCC applied its efforts to some large companies that produced fabrics for the federal government. Despite resistance from white employers and their white employees, simple economics won out. Companies couldn't afford to lose federal government business.

The construction industry was also notorious for discriminatory practices. Even though national unions supported the Civil Rights Act, the same was not true for skilled trades at the local level, particularly in the North and West. There, white union members refused admission to blacks. In Oakland, California,

Construction crews on the Gateway Arch in St. Louis included black workers—but only after a federal court ordered unions to comply with federal law.

for example, federally funded construction crews for a new post office in a black neighborhood had no black electricians, plumbers, or sheet metal workers. In St. Louis, allowing black workers on the Gateway Arch project took an OFCC lawsuit and federal court injunction to force unions to comply.

LEGALLY TESTING THE WATERS

By the end of the 1960s, challenges to affirmative action policies came before federal courts. One was *Quarles v. Philip*

Morris, Inc., in 1968. After the Civil Rights Act went into effect, some black employees at Philip Morris, a Virginia tobacco company, transferred from what had been considered "black-jobs" in the janitorial department to departments with better-paying jobs that before had been open only to whites. The issue was that promotions depended most on seniority—how long the employee had worked in the department. The company failed to count the time that black employees had worked in the janitorial department toward their seniority. Black employees Douglas Quarles and Ephraim Briggs sued the company and the tobacco workers union in a Virginia district court. The court ordered the company to revise its seniority policies.

Another early case concerned job requirements for pre-viously "white jobs." The Duke Power Company in North Carolina did allow black applicants for jobs previously held only by whites. However, the company required a high school diploma or a standardized general intelligence test as a con-dition of employment. The company showed no relationship between these requirements and actual job performance. In 1971, the U.S. Supreme Court ruled in *Griggs v. Duke Power Co.* that the practice was biased because blacks had a hard time meeting the qualifications.

These early cases were just the beginning of challenges to affirmative action policies put forth by the federal government.

A NEW PRESIDENT

As vice president in the administration of Dwight D. Eisenhower, Richard M. Nixon chaired the President's Committee on Government Contracts. In 1955, he met with leaders of business, industry, and labor unions, as well as government agencies that hired them under federal contracts. He also met with people from organizations working against discrimination in employment. The purpose of these

In 1957, Vice President Richard Nixon met with Dr. Martin Luther King Jr. *(left)* and Secretary of Labor James P. Mitchell to discuss labor policies.

meetings was to explain federal government fair employment practices. Nixon emphasized problems not so much with hiring practices, but with a lack of minority advancement after getting a job. (He appears to have overlooked discriminatory hiring practices in the petroleum, railroad, and construction industries.)

By 1969, Nixon occupied the White House. As president, he faced a delicate political balancing act. His close election had depended on support from white Democrats in the South—voters who traditionally opposed civil rights activities. Nixon also had to come up with a way to ensure a fair hiring policy that would serve as a middle ground between those advocated by leaders such as former vice president Hubert Humphrey on the pro side and George Wallace, a die-hard segregationist from Alabama who was against affirmative action.

As president, Nixon called for "law and order" in response to race riots in urban areas, as well as white opposition to forced school busing programs and integrated schools. He also called for technical assistance and loan guarantees to encourage blacks to start or expand their own businesses.

THE PHILADELPHIA PLAN

The U.S. Department of Labor worked to promote equal job opportunity, especially in the construction industry, which had been well known for racial discrimination. The industry offered high-paying jobs, but workers were predominantly white. The department sought to guarantee fair practices in minority hiring by asking contractors and labor unions to voluntarily remove obstacles for black applicants.

Progress in this area was slow. In an attempt to speed up the process, the Department of Labor adopted the Philadelphia Plan, which was based on a plan that had been created but never used during the Johnson administration. The executive order required federal contractors to make a "good faith" effort to hire minorities in accordance with a range of percentages of African Americans in their workforces by a specific date. Although the plan included specific goals and timetables, officials carefully kept from using the word "quotas" to describe them.

First used in September 1969 for federal contractors in Philadelphia, the plan met with controversy and fierce opposition. However, in February 1970, the department imposed the plan on federally funded construction projects in other cities unless local officials came up with their own policies for minority hiring. Many cities developed their own ways to encourage equal opportunity agreements among contractors, labor unions, and minority organizations. Some applied the plans to private construction, as well as federally funded projects. The OFCC programs helped coordinate and improve management of these plans.

Chapter 3

ON THE JOB

Federal affirmative action policies applied to companies under contract with the federal government. The policies outlined whom the contractors could do business with. They also affected business decisions about hiring and firing. The policies, however, did not go unchallenged.

In several important cases, the Supreme Court further shaped affirmative action practices. In different cases, the Court ruled that:

- The requirement to hire minority businesses did not hurt nonminority businesses.
- Layoffs based on race discriminated against nonminorities.
- Hiring quotas could be used to make up for prior discrimination.
- A city that tried to be fair to minorities in promotion decisions discriminated against white and Hispanic candidates.
- Women should earn the same pay rates as men in similar jobs, even if the jobs were not exactly the same.
- Employers could use gender as one of the factors in hiring decisions.

In 1977, the Public Works Employment Act required public works projects that received federal funds to use 10 percent of the money to buy supplies and services from minority-owned businesses. Even though 10 percent didn't sound like much, it represented a lot of money to contractors who competed for those jobs.

H. Earl Fullilove, a contractor who lost business because of the new law, sued Secretary of Commerce Philip M. Klutznick. He said the law financially harmed him and other contractors, and that the law violated the equal protection clause of the Fourteenth Amendment to the U.S. Constitution. The Fourteenth Amendment states, in part, "No state shall make or enforce any law which shall abridge the privileges...of citizens of the United States...nor deny to any person within its jurisdiction the equal protection of the laws."

On July 2, 1980, the U.S. Supreme Court found that Congress had acted within its power under both the spending power and commerce clauses of the Constitution. The Court said the law did not violate rights of nonminority contractors. It also said that because the act was meant to make up for an unfair situation, Congress did not have to act in a "colorblind" manner.

WHO GOES FIRST?

Racial tension in Jackson, Mississippi, in the late 1970s and early 1980s led to a collective bargaining agreement that ended up in the Supreme Court. At issue were layoffs based on seniority. An agreement between the teachers' union and the Jackson Board of Education said that if layoffs became necessary, teachers with the most seniority would keep their jobs.

Philip Klutznick *(left)*, with University of Colorado president Arnold Weber, in 1982. Klutznick was the defendant in an affirmative action lawsuit in 1977.

However, minority teachers had fairly recently been added to school faculties under affirmative action policies. If the school board fired teachers according to seniority, a lopsided percentage of minority teachers would lose their jobs. Gains made under affirmative action would be erased. In consideration of that fact, the agreement said that layoffs of minorities would keep the same percentage of minority faculty in place that had existed at the time of the layoff.

Layoffs, in fact, became necessary. The board kept some minority teachers with less seniority than some white

The justices of the Burger court, in the case of *Wygant v. Jackson Board of Education*, ruled that race-based layoffs went against the equal protection clause of the U.S. Consitution.

teachers who lost their jobs. Wendy Wygant was one of the nonminority teachers laid off. She sued, saying that race-based layoffs violated the Fourteenth Amendment's equal protection clause.

On May 19, 1986, the U.S. Supreme Court ruled that since Wygant's layoff was based on her race, it violated the clause. The Court further said, "Denial of a future employment opportunity is not as (bad) as loss of an existing job." In effect, the ruling meant that benefits to minorities could not justify harm to nonminorities.

A NUMBERS GAME

Improving employment opportunities for those who had previously experienced discrimination seemed like a good idea. However, in practice, employers had trouble with numbers. Should the new opportunities meet set numbers or percentages of minority personnel?

The Alabama Department of Public Safety brought attention to the issue. The department simply refused to hire blacks. As of 1970, not a single minority state trooper had been hired. In 1972, the district court ordered a hiring quota and told the department to quit discriminating in employment and promotion. However, by 1979, black troopers were stuck in entry-level positions. None held the rank of corporal or higher.

In 1983, the district court ordered a promotion plan. It required the promotion of one black trooper for every white promoted if qualified applicants were available. The policy would remain in place until 25 percent of the troopers in each upper rank were black.

In *United States v. Paradise* in 1987, the U.S. Supreme Court upheld the use of quotas as one of the few ways of fighting the department's racism. The Court said the plan did not impose an "absolute bar" to white promotion. The Court also said the plan was required because of the department's "long and shameful record of delay and resistance" to past Court decisions.

Alabama state troopers on the job in 2010. Two decades earlier, the Supreme Court had ruled in favor of hiring and promotion quotas for the state's department of public safety.

THE TROUBLE WITH NUMBERS

Despite allowing quotas in *Paradise*, the Court limited affirmative action practices in other cases. For instance, in 1983, the city council of Richmond, Virginia, passed a regulation that set aside 30 percent of construction funds for businesses owned by minorities. The J. A. Croson Company lost a contract because of the new rule and sued the city.

The Supreme Court ruled in 1989 in the company's favor. The decision called affirmative action a "highly suspect tool." It also said that affirmative action was unconstitutional unless unfair practices were "widespread throughout a particular industry." The Court said past racial bias was no excuse for imposing quotas. Justice Sandra Day O'Connor wrote, "The dream of a Nation of equal citizens in a society where race is irrelevant to personal opportunity and achievement would be lost in a mosaic of shifting preferences based on inherently unmeasurable claims of past wrongs."

In another case, the Court considered the constitutionality of the Department of Transportation's practice of giving money to contractors who hired small businesses controlled by "socially and economically disadvantaged individuals."

Adarand Constructors, Inc., submitted the lowest bid to provide guardrails for a federal highway project. The terms of the contract included additional payment to the prime contractor if it hired small businesses controlled by "Black Americans, Hispanic Americans, Native Americans, Asian Pacific Americans, and other minorities." A similar clause appeared in most federal contracts. Adarand Constructors was not certified as a minority business.

Instead of taking Adarand's lowest bid, the prime contractor hired Gonzales Construction Company, which had minority status. Adarand Constructors sued, saying it would have got the job if the government had not offered extra payment for hiring Gonzales.

In *Adarand Constructors, Inc. v. Peña,* which was decided on June 12, 1995, the Court ruled in favor of the plaintiff. It said the case required "strict scrutiny review," since the situation gave favored treatment to one class of people. Strict scrutiny meant the Court would presume the government practice invalid unless the government showed it had the right to regulate the situation.

The Court said the statute in question seemed to assume that those who benefit from special treatment are less qualified simply based on their race. The Court said that race is not a reason to assume a person is disadvantaged. A minority opinion issued by Justices Antonin Scalia and Clarence Thomas said affirmative action should be completely banned.

"MEND IT, DON'T END IT"

A month after the *Adarand* decision, President Bill Clinton spoke about affirmative action at the National Archives in Washington, D.C. He said, "Let us remember always that finding common ground as we move toward the twenty-first century depends fundamentally on our shared commitment to equal opportunity for all Americans."

Clinton reaffirmed the need for affirmative action because of continued discrimination in the nation. "Affirmative action remains a useful tool for widening economic and educational opportunity," he said.

MINORITY STATUS IN 1995

In his "Mend It, Don't End It" speech at the National Archives in Washington, D.C., President Bill Clinton encouraged continued affirmative action policies because of the status of minorities at the time. Points he emphasized included:

- The unemployment rate for African Americans was twice that of whites.
- Women still made only 72 percent of men's income for comparable jobs.
- The average income for a Hispanic woman with a college degree was less than the average income of a white man with a high school diploma.
- According to the recently completed report of the Glass Ceiling Commission, sponsored by Republican members of Congress, only 0.6 percent of senior management positions in the nation's largest companies were held by African Americans, 0.4 percent by Hispanic Americans, and 0.3 percent by Asian Americans; women held between 3 and 5 percent of these positions. White men made up 43 percent of the workforce, but they held 95 percent of these jobs.
- The Chicago Federal Reserve Bank reported that black home loan applicants were more than twice as likely to be denied credit as whites with the same qualifications.

He also said affirmative action did not mean preference of the unqualified over the qualified. And it did not mean selection or rejection of any employee or student solely on the basis of race or gender without regard to merit.

Clinton countered the argument that affirmative action discriminated against whites. "Last year alone, the federal government received more than ninety thousand complaints of employment discrimination based on race, ethnicity, or gender," he said. "Less than 3 percent were for reverse discrimination."

Clinton praised the U.S. Army for emphasizing education and training, which ensured a wide pool of qualified

President Bill Clinton praised the "colorblind" practices of the U.S. Army, which ensured a large pool of qualified candidates for every job regardless of race.

candidates for every level of promotion. The approach, he said, "has given us the most racially diverse and best qualified military in our history."

He also applauded the Small Business Administration for increasing loans to qualified minorities by 66 percent and loans to qualified women by more than 80 percent without decreasing loans to white men.

Acknowledging that affirmative action had often been imperfect, he said it should be changed instead of abandoned. "We should have a simple slogan," he said. "Mend it, but don't end it."

In a White House memorandum the same day as his speech, Clinton called for elimination of any program that:

- Created a quota
- Created preferences for unqualified individuals
- Created reverse discrimination
- Continued after its equal opportunity purposes had been achieved

LETTING IN WOMEN

The Transportation Agency in Santa Clara, California, had an affirmative action plan that sought to bring women into skilled jobs previously held only by men. All of its 238 skilled workers were men. Under the plan, the agency promoted Diane Joyce to road dispatcher. A male applicant, Paul Johnson, also met qualifications for the job—and had, in fact, scored higher in the evaluation process. However, the agency took Joyce's gender into account in making the promotion decision. Johnson sued.

On March 25, 1987, in *Johnson v. Santa Clara County Transportation Agency*, the Supreme Court ruled in favor of the agency. The Court said that the agency could use gender as one of several factors to choose among qualified candidates, especially when there was a statistical imbalance of male and female employees. The Court held that the agency's affirmative action plan created no absolute barrier to men.

Chapter 4

ON CAMPUS

Many affirmative action plans sought to rid the workplace of discrimination. Others focused on discrimination in education, particularly at the college level. Blacks and other minorities who applied to the nation's colleges and universities often got rejections based on race.

In an effort to correct those practices, many schools set goals or quotas to increase the number of minority students admitted. In some cases, that meant some white applicants were denied admission in favor of minority students with lower grades or test scores.

EQUAL PROTECTION OF THE LAW

A landmark decision by the U.S. Supreme Court, *Regents of the University of California v. Bakke,* addressed this issue in 1978. In order to make up for past discrimination against minorities in the field of medicine, the University of California Medical School at Davis had adopted an affirmative action plan that saved sixteen spots in each new class of one hundred students for "Blacks, Chicanos, Asians, and American Indians." A white man named Allan Bakke unsuccessfully applied for admission to the school. He applied a second time, and again he was denied admission. Both times, Bakke's grades and test scores were higher than many of the minority students who were accepted.

Reporters follow Allan Bakke after his first day at the University of California Medical School at Davis in 1978. The school admitted Bakke after he won a case before the U.S. Supreme Court.

Bakke sued the university, charging that his rejections were based solely on his race. The question before the Court was whether the medical school's affirmative action policy violated the Fourteenth Amendment's equal protection clause and/or the Civil Rights Act of 1964.

The Court's ruling had several parts. First, the Court said that strict racial quota plans violated the Civil Rights Act. Second, the Court said affirmative action policies that led to reverse discrimination were unfair. Third, it ruled that admitting minority students with lower grades and scores than a white applicant violated the Fourteenth Amendment. The Court ordered the university to abandon its quota system and admit Bakke.

On the other hand, the Court allowed race as a factor in admissions policies to promote diversity, especially to make up for past discriminatory practices. The opportunities for minorities, however, could not come at the expense of majority students.

DAWN DOWNEY'S STORY

Dawn Downey, an African American woman, entered Pomona College in 1969 as part of the liberal arts college's first affirmative action class. In keeping with the federal government's policy to ban discrimination at colleges that received federal funding, the Claremont, California, institution had expanded its recruitment activities to places where minority students went to school. Pomona kept its high entry standards but simply added some new recruiting locations.

"I don't know what their goal was," Downey said, "but a certain percentage of the freshman class had to be students of color."

In addition, Downey received a nearly full scholarship. "Pomona is a wealthy school," she said, "and they dedicated funds for minority scholarships. I graduated with only a couple thousand dollars of student loan debt."

After graduate school, Downey became associate director of admissions at the University of Kansas. "I could attribute my job to affirmative action," she said. "I was in charge of programs the admissions office created to recruit minority students, and the recruitment programs were required because of affirmative action."

RACE AS A FACTOR
IN ADMISSIONS

In 1996, a black businessman from Sacramento, California, was busy working against affirmative action in California universities. Ward Connerly chaired the Board of Regents of the University of California system. He was no fan of affirmative action, and he pushed to end race-based admissions. He also became a spokesperson for Proposition 209, which called for a stop to all preferences based on race or gender in the state.

In November 1996, California voters approved the proposition 54 percent to 46 percent. (Two years later, a similar initiative stopped affirmative action practices in the state of Washington.) After the California ballot issue passed, the Fifth U.S. Court of Appeals seemed to agree with voters when ruling in *Hopwood v. Texas*.

The University of Texas School of Law was one of the best in the nation, so competition for admission was fierce. The school could easily enroll only white, straight-A students. However, it sought to foster diversity in its student body.

Cheryl Hopwood, a white graduate of California State University at Sacramento, applied for admission to the University of Texas School of Law in 1992. Hopwood worked thirty to forty hours a week to pay her way through college. At the same time, she cared for her baby, who was born with cerebral palsy, as well as volunteering for the Big Brothers/ Big Sisters Program. Her qualifications—a 3.8 grade point average and a good score on the Law School Admission Test (LSAT)—placed her higher than at least eighty-five of the black and Hispanic applicants the school admitted. The admissions policy used an index system that required white applicants to score in the top 9 percent of those taking the LSAT. Hispanics needed scores only in the top 25 percent.

The law school denied Hopwood admission, and she sued the university for unfair racial preferences in admissions. On March 18, 1996, the Fifth U.S. Court of Appeals ruled in favor of Hopwood, rejecting the idea that educational diversity was a "compelling state interest." The school's affirmative action plan was suspended.

In essence, the appeals court ruling in *Hopwood* determined that part of the U.S. Supreme Court's decision in *Bakke* was unconstitutional. The Supreme Court declined to hear *Hopwood* on appeal, however, thus letting the lower court's ruling stand.

Shortly after the ruling, the Texas attorney general told all Texas public universities to use race-neutral policies for admission to their schools. Because the appeals court had jurisdiction in Texas, Louisiana, and Mississippi, the ruling also banned affirmative action in college admissions in those states as well.

ONE FLORIDA

In late 1999, then Florida governor Jeb Bush issued an executive order called One Florida. With the order, Bush hoped to close the gap in opportunities and incomes between whites and minorities. He also wanted to avoid another legal ruling like the one that banned affirmative action in Texas. To complicate matters, California's Ward Connerly had set his sights on Florida for a public vote against affirmative action. Bush wanted to avoid a severe ban on affirmative action in Florida like the one that passed in California.

One Florida banned race as a factor in college admissions. It did, however, give breaks to poor students in college admissions. Instead of granting college admission based on race, One Florida provided that all high school students in the top 20 percent of their graduating class were guaranteed acceptance to at least one of the ten state universities.

Many in the black community were outraged, but some black leaders agreed that One Florida might give more opportunities to poor students. And, after all, a large percentage of underprivileged students were black. The leaders didn't like the idea of getting rid of affirmative action altogether, though. Despite objections, the Florida legislature approved the plan.

CHANGING THE COURT'S MIND

In another landmark case concerning college admissions, *Grutter v. Bollinger*, the Supreme Court threw out the earlier decision in *Hopwood*. Barbara Grutter, a white Michigan resident, applied for admission to the University of Michigan Law School. The school rejected her application despite a 3.8 undergraduate GPA and a high score on the LSAT. She sued Lee Bollinger, president of the university, for violating her rights under the Fourteenth Amendment and the Civil Rights Act.

The law school had used race as a factor in its admissions decisions. However, the defendant said, the use of race was necessary to achieve diversity among its student body. Bollinger and the school maintained that all applications were carefully and individually reviewed with an eye toward considering all factors that contribute to diversity, with race as only one factor.

Barbara Grutter (in 2001) lost her lawsuit when the Supreme Court ruled that the University of Michigan Law School could use affirmative action to achieve a racially diverse student body.

In a decision announced in 2003, the U.S. Supreme Court agreed with the school's argument. The Court said the university's admissions practices did not violate Grutter's equal protection under the law. The Court also said the school had a compelling interest in ensuring diversity among its students due to educational benefits that result from it. In the decision, Justice Sandra Day O'Connor wrote, "The Law School's race-conscious admissions program does not unduly harm nonminority applicants."

In changing the opinion in *Hopwood,* the Court went back to the decision in *Bakke,* which allowed race as a factor in admissions. The *Grutter* ruling meant that using race as a significant factor, but not one that by itself determined acceptance, was neutral enough.

Another case that involved the University of Michigan was announced the same day as *Grutter.* In *Gratz v. Bollinger,* the Court told the university to change its undergraduate admission practices. The school's affirmative action plan used a point system to compare applicants and gave extra points to minority students. It discontinued the point system after the Court ruled.

The Court's rulings in *Grutter* and *Gratz* had little effect on discrimination in higher education. At the time, only 10 to 15 percent of colleges and universities had competitive admissions in the first place, according to John W. Johnson and Robert P. Green Jr. in *Historical Guides to Controversial Issues in America: Affirmative Action.*

WHAT ABOUT HIGH SCHOOLS?

Change was on its way. On July 1, 2005, Supreme Court Justice Sandra Day O'Connor retired. And on September 3 of the same year, Chief Justice William Rehnquist died of thyroid cancer. Two new judges, Samuel Alito and John W. Roberts, took their places. The new Court soon heard its first affirmative action cases.

Two Supreme Court verdicts, issued in 2007, affected the use of affirmative action at the high school level. In *Parents*

Involved in Community Schools v. Seattle School District, the public school district let students attend any high school they wanted. But some schools had more applicants than room. The district used race as a reason to admit some and not others based on keeping a ratio of 40 percent white and 60 percent nonwhite students in each building.

A parent group sued the district. The Supreme Court said that the system was unconstitutional. The Court said the district's plan was not targeted toward educational benefit from racial diversity. Instead, the district simply tried to maintain racial balance.

A similar situation existed in *Meredith v. Jefferson County Board of Education.* The Jefferson County school district in Louisville, Kentucky, had followed a court order to integrate its schools, but the order expired in 2000. As in Seattle, students got to choose their schools, but some schools had less space than applicants. Decisions about who could attend were based on where the student lived, the amount of room in the school, and pure chance.

In an effort to maintain racial diversity, Austin Johnson (with his mother, Deborah Stallworth) was denied admission to Central High School in Louisville, Kentucky. On appeal in 2006, Johnson was admitted.

However, in an effort to maintain racial diversity, the district also considered the student's race.

The Supreme Court ruled the district's policy unconstitutional. In the opinion, Chief Justice John Roberts wrote, "The way to stop discrimination on the basis of race is to stop discriminating on the basis of race."

The Court said that the previous rulings in *Grutter* and *Gratz* did not apply to the situation for two reasons. One, school officials failed to individually consider each applicant. And two, the district limited its idea of diversity only to "black" and "other."

Chapter 5

RECONSIDERING AFFIRMATIVE ACTION

A s the courts narrowed the focus of affirmative action, more issues arose. An amount of backlash came in the form of court rulings that tightened the reins on "how much was too much" in terms of equity programs. More than that, the American public was organizing and speaking out more against affirmative action mandates.

PASSING THE TEST

In 2003, the New Haven Fire Department in Connecticut had fifteen openings to fill. Seven firefighters would be promoted to captain, and eight to lieutenant. According to the city's promotion procedures, firefighters interested in the promotions took a written civil service test. They also completed an oral exam.

According to an agreement between the city and the firefighters union, results were weighted. That meant that the written test counted for 60 percent of an applicant's score, and the oral exam counted for 40 percent. The contract also provided that an applicant needed a score of 70 percent to pass. The city's charter required each opening to be filled by one of the three firefighters with the highest scores.

Frank Ricci *(center)* celebrates with fellow firefighters after the U.S. Supreme Court ruled in their favor in a 2009 reverse discrimination case.

Seventy-seven firefighters took the lieutenant tests. The applicants included forty-three whites, nineteen blacks, and fifteen Hispanics. Of the forty-one who took the captain tests, twenty-five were white, eight were black, and eight were Hispanic. Scores revealed uneven results. Only half as many minority applicants got passing scores compared to the percentage of white candidates who passed. On the lieutenant exam, 58 percent of whites passed, 32 percent of blacks passed, and 20 percent of Hispanics passed. On the captain exam, 64 percent of whites passed. Only 38 percent each of black and Hispanic applicants passed. According to the city charter, all those eligible for promotion to lieutenant were white. Again, for captain, no black applicant made the list.

The New Haven Civil Service Board was asked to certify the test results. The board feared that using the test scores would violate the Civil Rights Act if the tests were shown to be racially biased. After several hearings, the board refused to certify the test. The city threw out the test, and no one was promoted.

GROUPS OPPOSED TO AFFIRMATIVE ACTION

In the years since the first affirmative action plans went into effect, several organizations have opposed them. Among them:

- The Center for Individual Rights (CIR), a Washington, D.C., nonprofit public interest law firm dedicated to enforcing constitutional limits on state and federal power
- The American Civil Rights Institute (ACRI), the California-based organization led by Ward Connerly that campaigned to overturn affirmative action policies through statewide votes. Its slogan on its website says, "Race has no place in American life or law"
- The Center for Equal Opportunity (CEO), an organization based in Falls Church, Virginia, that supports an end to racial preferences in university admissions
- The National Association of Scholars (NAS), a group of university faculty members who oppose race-conscious policies

Frank Ricci had spent eleven years as a firefighter with the New Haven department. He applied for a promotion to lieutenant and took a written test that placed him sixth among the seventy-seven other candidates for eight openings. When the department threw out the test, Ricci and other applicants who would have qualified for promotion sued the city and its mayor, John DeStefano Jr.

The suit charged reverse discrimination. It said that throwing out the test discriminated against the white and Hispanic firefighters because of their race. The city said if they had used the test results, they would have faced being charged with adopting a practice that discriminated against minorities.

The U.S. Supreme Court handed down its opinion on June 29, 2009. The Court ruled that the city had indeed discriminated against the white and Hispanic firefighters by throwing out the test. The Court said that the city had to show strong evidence that if it had not taken the action, the city would have been accountable for discriminating against minorities. However, the Court said, the city had not met that requirement.

THE COURT OF PUBLIC OPINION

Outside the courtroom, public opinion began trending away from affirmative action, due in part to the efforts of Ward Connerly, the founder and chair of the Civil Rights Institute who had led the California affirmative action ban

Civil Rights Institute founder Ward Connerly *(left)* waits to see if Initiative 424, which would eliminate affirmative action in Nebraska, would pass in 2008.

with Proposition 209. Connerly had succeeded in the adoption of similar bans in the states of Washington and Michigan. He next tried to get similar initiatives on the ballot in the November 2008 general elections in Arizona, Colorado, Missouri, Nebraska, and Oklahoma.

Although Connerly failed to get an affirmative action ban on the ballots in Arizona, Missouri, and Oklahoma, he did get the issue before voters in Colorado and Nebraska. Colorado voters rejected the proposal, but Nebraska voters passed Initiative 424 as an amendment to the state constitution. The initiative read, "The state shall not discriminate against, or grant preferential treatment to, any individual or group on the basis of race, sex, color, ethnicity, or national origin in the operation of public employment, public education, or public contracting."

The ban applies only to state agencies and cities, and only if eligibility for federal funding requires affirmative action "if ineligibility would result in a loss of federal funds to the state."

BACK TO SCHOOL

In the face of growing popular opinion against affirmative action, the courts weren't quite through with the issue. Shortly after the *Hopwood* decision, Texas public universities adopted race-neutral admission policies. The following year,

Abigail Fisher talks to reporters outside the Supreme Court building in 2012. In 2013, the Court ruled that Fisher had wrongfully been denied university admission because of affirmative action.

the Texas legislature required the University of Texas to admit all Texas high school graduates who ranked in the top 10 percent of their high school classes.

University officials noticed that the racial composition of the student body did not match the state's population. They changed their race-neutral admission policy. After admitting the "top ten percenters," the school used race as a factor in admissions.

Abigail Fisher, a white woman who was not in her high school's top 10 percent, applied for admission to the university. The university denied her application. She sued, saying the school's use of race in admissions decisions violated her rights. Lawyers for the university argued that the use of race was a way to achieve diversity to enhance students' educational experience.

The district court ruled in favor of the university. So did the U.S. Court of Appeals for the Fifth Circuit. Fisher appealed to the U.S. Supreme Court. The Court considered whether the equal protection clause of the Fourteenth Amendment allows the use of race in making admissions decisions.

The Supreme Court ruled in Fisher's favor in June 2013. It said that race could be used as a factor in admissions, but only under the "strict scrutiny" level of judicial review. Under strict scrutiny, the Court had to assume the university's actions invalid unless it showed a compelling interest that it had a right to regulate admissions based on race.

The Court sent the case back to the Fifth Circuit, saying its ruling was incorrect. It told the lower court to further review the matter to determine whether the policies were necessary to achieve the benefits of diversity and that no race-neutral alternative would provide the same benefits.

BACK TO MICHIGAN

By 2008, eighteen states had laws, constitutional amendments, or other government policies that banned race-based admissions for higher education. In effect, the state actions got rid of affirmative action in employment or education. One such constitutional amendment, in Michigan, arrived at the U.S. Supreme Court for judgment.

In 2006, Michigan voters had approved Proposal 2 with the support of Ward Connerly. The proposal amended the state constitution and banned discrimination against or preferential treatment toward individuals in public education, government contracting, and public employment on the basis of race, sex, ethnicity, or national origin. Two years later, a Michigan district court said the amendment was constitutional, but on appeal to the Sixth Circuit Court, it was declared unconstitutional.

The circuit court said the amendment violated a political-restructuring doctrine, which holds that the equal protection clause subtly places special burdens on the ability of minority groups to get passage of beneficial laws. The doctrine came from a 1969 lawsuit, *Hunter v. Erickson*. There, voters in Akron, Ohio, repealed a fair housing ordinance that banned discrimination in the sale or lease of real property. They then passed an amendment that made it harder to pass antidiscrimination laws in the future. The U.S. Supreme Court said the action was unconstitutional because it restructured the political process and made it harder for minorities to avoid discrimination.

The Supreme Court again applied the political-restructuring doctrine in *Washington v. Seattle Sch. Dist. No. 1* in 1982.

Supporters of affirmative action rally in front of the U.S. Supreme Court building during a case against Michigan's constitutional amendment that banned affirmative action in education and employment.

Voters passed a state initiative that prohibited school busing for desegregation but allowed busing for other purposes. The Court said the initiative violated the doctrine because the government's action dealt with racial issues.

It took seven years for *Schuette v. Coalition to Defend Affirmative Action, Integration and Immigration Rights and Right for Equality by Any Means Necessary* to reach the U.S. Supreme Court. The Court agreed to hear the case in 2013. Its focus was whether a state violates the equal protection clause by amending its constitution to prohibit race- and sex-based discrimination or preferential treatment in public university admissions decisions.

The courts will eventually determine whether affirmative action will fade away or remain a force in American life. What began as a temporary measure may outlive its use, or discriminatory practices may continue and need remedy.

HAS AFFIRMATIVE ACTION WORKED?

Despite growing opposition to affirmative action policies, they seem to have made a difference in schools and the workplace. Stephen Carter, an African American Yale University law professor, analyzed the effects of affirmative action in the thirty years since the *Bakke* decision. Writing in 2008 in the *New York Times*, Carter noted, "It's true that, nowadays, some of the data on racial progress are rosy, and deserving of celebration."

Carter cited the U.S. Census Bureau's finding that between 1998 and 2008, the number of black adults with advanced degrees had nearly doubled. Other statistics included:

- More than half a million more black students are in college today than in the early 1990s.
- In the past twenty years, the median income of black families increased more than 16 percent.
- The black-white gap in test scores has narrowed.
- The black middle class has never been larger.
- He also celebrated the nomination of Barack Obama as the first African American candidate for president.

Still, he said that among African Americans, "the gap between the well-off and the poor is growing." One in three black students still failed to finish high school, and nearly all of those are poor. He said that affirmative action "did not fundamentally improve the plight of the poorest Americans of color."

Merrill Middle School
Media Center
Oshkosh, WI

In the majority opinion in the 2003 *Grutter* case, Supreme Court Justice Sandra Day O'Connor noted that, at the time of the ruling, it had been twenty-five years since the Court first ruled in favor of affirmative action measures. Then she added, on a seemingly hopeful note, "We expect that twenty-five years from now, the use of racial preferences will no longer be necessary to further (that) interest."

TIMELINE

March 6, 1961   President John F. Kennedy signs Executive Order 10925.

July 2, 1964 President Lyndon Johnson signs the Civil Rights Act.

June 4, 1965 President Johnson defines "affirmative action" in a speech at Howard University.

September 24, 1965 President Johnson signs Executive Order 11246, which enforces affirmative action.

October 13, 1967 President Johnson issues Executive Order 11375, which amends Executive Order 11246 to include a ban on gender bias.

1969 President Richard Nixon issues the Philadelphia Order, defining goals and timetables for increasing minority employment in the construction industry.

1970 The U.S. Labor Department issues Order Number 4, regarding the construction industry.

1976 The U.S. Supreme Court ruling comes down in *Washington County v. Gunther.*

1977 The Supreme Court rules in *Dothard v. Rawlinson* regarding discrimination against women based on height and weight.

June 28, 1978   The Supreme Court ruling in *Regents of the University of California v. Bakke* strikes down strict quotas.

July 2, 1980 The Supreme Court ruling in *Fullilove v. Klutznick* determines that some "modest" quotas are constitutional.

May 19, 1986 The Supreme Court ruling in *Wygant v. Jackson Board of Education* concerns the constitutionality of teacher layoffs predicated by affirmative action.

February 25, 1987 The Supreme Court orders the State of Alabama Department of Public Safety to meet specific racial quotas in hiring black state troopers.

March 25, 1987 The Supreme Court ruling in *Johnson v. Santa Clara County Transportation Agency* upholds the use of gender as a factor in choosing among qualified candidates.

January 23, 1989 The Supreme Court ruling in *City of Richmond v. Croson* requires "strict scrutiny" of affirmative action programs at state and local levels.

July 19, 1995 President Bill Clinton issues guidelines on affirmative action, calling for removal of programs that create reverse discrimination.

October 15, 2013 Supreme Court hearings begin on Michigan's voter-backed ban on using race as a factor in college admissions.

GLOSSARY

AFFIRMATIVE ACTION A plan, program, or policy that makes an active effort to improve the employment or educational opportunities for minorities and women.

APPEAL With regard to the law, when a case is brought before a higher court, to either affirm or reject a lower court's ruling.

BIAS A strong preference for someone or something, to the point that actions are unfair to others.

BLACKFACE Theatrical makeup used by white entertainers in minstrel and vaudeville song-and-dance acts. Actors applied burnt cork and cocoa butter or black grease paint to portray stereotypical black characters.

COMPELLING INTEREST A legal concept that lets a government regulate something.

CONTRACTOR A person or business that provides goods or services under contract, as opposed to an employee.

DIVERSITY Having various people of different races, cultures, and beliefs together in one place working toward one ideal.

ENVISION To picture in one's mind; to imagine.

GOOD FAITH EFFORT An attempt to meet minority hiring or contract goals by exhausting all available methods.

INTEGRATION Blending people of different races and genders in such places as schools and workplaces.

JIM CROW LAWS A series of state laws first enacted in the South in the 1880s that officially separated black and white races, with favor toward whites.

LANDMARK CASE An important lawsuit that establishes a new law and serves as a guide for decisions in cases with a similar situation.

MAJORITY A group of people that has more members than other groups, and therefore having more power.

MINORITY A smaller group that has less power.

PLAINTIFF A person who in a court of law accuses someone else of having done something illegal.

QUOTA A specific number or percentage used as a goal or requirement, such as used in systems for hiring minority applicants.

REVERSE DISCRIMINATION Showing bias against whites or men in favor of blacks or women.

SCRUTINY The act of giving something extra-careful attention for review or judgment.

SEGREGATION The act of keeping people of different races or genders separate in such places as schools and workplaces.

SENIORITY The amount of time an employee has worked for a company or department compared with the time other workers have been there.

American Association for Affirmative Action (AAAA)
888 16th Street NW, Suite 800
Washington, DC 20006
(800) 252-8952
Website: http://www.affirmativeaction.org
The AAAA is a nonprofit organization of individuals and
  organizations dedicated to nurturing understanding
  of affirmative action. It offers training and educational
  programs that promote professional growth and develop-
  ment of its members.

Canadian Civil Liberties Association (CCLA)
215 Spadina Avenue, Suite 210
Toronto, ON M5T 2C7
Canada
(416) 363-0321
Website: http://ccla.org
The Canadian Civil Liberties Association's equality program seeks to promote fairness and equality in Canada
  regardless of disability, gender, sexual orientation, race,
  ethnicity, religion, age, socioeconomic status, and immigration status.

Canadian Federation of Students-Ontario (CFSO)
180 Bloor Street West, Suite 900
Toronto, ON M5S 2V6
Canada
(416) 925-3825
Website: http://cfsontario.ca/en/section/190
The Canadian Federation of Students-Ontario is an

organization of more than three hundred thousand members that supports affirmative action programs and policies in hiring practices and equal access to social services and opportunities.

Congress of Racial Equality (CORE)
National Headquarters
817 Broadway, 3rd Floor
New York, NY 10003
(800) 439-CORE (2673)
Website: http://core-online.org
CORE is a civil rights organization founded in 1942 in Chicago. Its history includes protests against Jim Crow laws in the 1940s, sit-ins in the 1950s, and freedom rides in the 1960s. Its mission is to establish the right for all people to determine their own destiny. It works to bring about equality for all people.

National Association for the Advancement of Colored People (NAACP)
National Headquarters
4805 Mt. Hope Drive
Baltimore, MD 21215
(877) NAACP98 (622-2798)
Website: http://www.naacp.org
The NAACP is a civil rights organization founded in 1909. Its mission is to ensure political, social, educational, and economic equality for all. It also seeks to eliminate racial hatred and discrimination.

National Organization for Women (NOW)
1100 H Street NW, Suite 300
Washington, DC 20005
(202) 628-8669
Website: http://www.now.org
NOW is an organization of feminist activists in the United States.
It was founded in 1966 to work toward equality for all women.
Its current goals include eliminating discrimination and
harassment in the workplace, as well as other social issues.

National Urban League
120 Wall Street
New York, NY 10005
(212) 528-5300
Website: http://nul.iamempowered.com
The Urban League seeks to "enable African Americans to
achieve economic self-reliance, parity, power, and civil
rights." It was founded as the Committee on Urban
Conditions Among Negroes in 1910. The following year,
it merged with the Committee for the Improvement of
Industrial Conditions Among Negroes and the National
League for the Protection of Colored Women to eventually
become the Urban League.

WEBSITES

Due to the changing nature of Internet links, Rosen
Publishing has developed an online list of websites related to
the subject of this book. This site is updated regularly. Please
use the following link to access the list:

http://www.rosenlinks.com/CCRM/Affirm

Aretha, David. *Martin Luther King Jr. and the 1963 March on Washington.* Greensboro, NC: Morgan Reynolds Publishing, 2014.

Behnken, Brian. *Fighting Their Own Battles: Mexican Americans, African Americans, and the Struggle for Civil Rights in Texas.* Chapel Hill, NC: University of North Carolina Press, 2011.

Booker, Simeon, and Carol McCabe. *Shocking the Conscience: A Reporter's Account of the Civil Rights Movement.* Jackson, MS: University Press of Mississippi, 2013.

Delmont, Matthew F. *The Nicest Kids in Town: American Bandstand, Rock 'n' Roll, and the Struggle for Civil Rights in 1950s Philadelphia.* Berkeley, CA: University of California Press, 2012.

Duru, N. Jeremi. *Advancing the Ball: Race, Reformation, and the Quest for Equal Coaching Opportunity in the NFL.* New York, NY: Oxford University Press USA, 2012.

Griffin, John Howard. *Black Like Me.* San Antonio, TX: Wings Press, 2010.

Jackson, Thomas F. *From Civil Rights to Human Rights: Martin Luther King, Jr., and the Struggle for Economic Justice.* Philadelphia, PA: University of Pennsylvania Press, 2009.

Kidd, Sue Monk. *The Secret Life of Bees.* New York, NY: Penguin Books, 2002.

Mack, Kenneth W., and E. Charles Guy-Uriel. *The New Black.* New York, NY: The New Press, 2013.

Mayer, Robert H. *When the Children Marched: The Birmingham Civil Rights Movement.* Berkeley Heights, NJ: Enslow Publishers, 2008.

McWhorter, Diane. *Carry Me Home: Birmingham, Alabama: The Climactic Battle of the Civil Rights Revolution.* New York, NY: Simon & Schuster, 2013.

Miller, Jake. *Sit-Ins and Freedom Rides.* New York, NY: Rosen Publishing, 2004.

Nolan, Han. *A Summer of Kings.* Boston, MA: HMH Books for Young Readers, 2012.

Osborne, Linda Barrett. *Miles to Go for Freedom: Segregation and Civil Rights in the Jim Crow Years.* New York, NY: Abrams Books for Young Readers, 2012.

Pastin, Amy, and Primo Levi. *DK Biography: Martin Luther King, Jr.* New York, NY: DK Children, 2004.

Povich, Lynn. *The Good Girls Revolt: How the Women of Newsweek Sued their Bosses and Changed the Workplace.* New York, NY: PublicAffairs, 2012.

Sandel, Michael J. *Justice: What's the Right Thing to Do?* New York, NY: Farrar, Straus and Giroux, 2010.

Whitt, Margaret Earley. *Short Stories of the Civil Rights Movement: An Anthology.* Athens, GA: University of Georgia Press, 2006.

Womack, Ytasha L. *Post Black: How a New Generation Is Redefining African American Identity.* Chicago, IL: Chicago Review Press, 2010.

Younge, Gary. *The Speech: The Story Behind Dr. Martin Luther King Jr.'s Dream.* Chicago, IL: Haymarket Books, 2013.

Borowski, Susan. "Affirmative Action and Reverse Discrimination: Walking the Fine Line." InsightintoDiversity.com, June 2012. Retrieved November 2, 2013 (http://www.insightintodiversity.com/affirmative-action-and-reverse-discrimination-walking-the-fine-line-susan-borowski).

Carter, Stephen L. "Affirmative Distraction." *New York Times,* July 6, 2008. Retrieved December 7, 2013 (http://www.nytimes.com/2008/07/06/opinion/06carter.html?pagewanted=all&_r=0).

Center for Individual Rights. "*Hopwood*: The First Victory in a Long War." July 23, 2013. Retrieved November 21, 2013 (http://www.cir-usa.org/cases/hopwood.html).

Clements, Phil, and Tony Spinks. *The Equal Opportunities Handbook: How to Recognize Diversity, Encourage Fairness, and Promote Anti-Discriminatory Practice.* Philadelphia, PA: Kogan Page, 2009.

Clinton, William Jefferson. "Mend It, Don't End It." Speech at the National Archives, July 1995. Retrieved December 6, 2013 (http://web.utk.edu/~mfitzge1/docs/374/MDE1995.pdf).

Dobbin, Frank. *Inventing Equal Opportunity.* Princeton, NJ: Princeton University Press, 2011.

Golland, David Hamilton. *Constructing Affirmative Action: The Struggle for Equal Employment Opportunity* (Civil Rights and the Struggle for Black Equality in the Twentieth Century). Lexington KY: University Press of Kentucky, 2011.

IIT Chicago-Kent College of Law. "*Griggs v. Duke Power Company.*" Oyez.org, 1970. Retrieved November 10, 2013 (http://www.oyez.org/cases/1970-1979/1970/1970_124).

Johnson, John W., and Robert P. Green, Jr. *Historical Guides to Controversial Issues in America: Affirmative Action.* Santa Barbara, CA: ABAC-CLIO, 2009.

Johnson, Lyndon B. "To Fulfill These Rights." Commencement address at Howard University, June 4, 1965. Retrieved September 5, 2013 (http://www.lbjlib.utexas.edu/johnson/archives.hom/speeches.hom/650604.asp).

Kennedy, Randall. *For Discrimination: Race, Affirmative Action, and the Law.* New York, NY: Pantheon Books, 2013.

Kilborn, Peter T. "Jeb Bush Roils Florida on Affirmative Action." *New York Times,* February 4, 2000. Retrieved December 2, 2013 (http://partners.nytimes.com/library/national/race/020400race-ra.html).

Legal.com/decisions. "*Quarles v. Philip Morris Inc.*" 1968. Retrieved November 10, 2013 (http://www.leagle.com/decision/1968784279FSupp505_1697).

McBride, Alex. "Expanding Civil Rights." PBS.org, December 2006. Retrieved November 20, 2013 (http://www.pbs.org/wnet/supremecourt/rights/landmark_regents.html).

Powers, Scott, and Luis Zaragoza. "10 Years In, 'One Florida' Posts Mixed Results for Minorities at Universities." *Orlando Sentinel,* April 10, 2010. Retrieved November 21, 2013 (http://articles.orlandosentinel.com/2010-04-10/news/os-one-florida-10-years-later-20100410_1_affirmative-action-florida-s-public-universities-graduates).

Sykes, Marquita. "The Origins of Affirmative Action." *National NOW Times,* August 1995. Retrieved November 2, 2013 (http://www.now.org/nnt/08-95/affirmhs.html).

UnderstandingRace.com. "The Beginning and the End of Affirmative Action." 2007. Retrieved November 1, 2013 (http://www.understandingrace.org/history/gov/begin_end_affirm.html).

University of California, Irvine. "A Brief History of Affirmative Action." Office of Equal Opportunity and Diversity. Retrieved September 4, 2013 (http://www.oeod.uci.edu/aa.html).

U.S. Department of Labor. "Nixon and Ford Administrations, 1969–1977." Retrieved November 2, 2013 (http://www.dol.gov/dol/aboutdol/history/dolchp07.htm).

Williams, Pete, and Daniel Arkin. "Supreme Court Takes on Affirmative Action in Michigan Ban." NBC News.com, October 21, 2013. Retrieved October 21, 2013.(http://usnews.nbcnews.com/_news/2013/10/15/20975390-supreme-court-takes-on-affirmative-action-in-michigan-ban-case?lite).

INDEX

A

Adarand Constructors, Inc. v. Peña,
   36–37
affirmative action
   in education, 42–52
   groups opposed to, 56
   historical backdrop, 8–17
   legislation, 18–28
   overview, 5–7
   present and future, 53–65
   and women, 6, 13, 21–22, 23, 29,
      38, 40–41, 44
   in the workplace, 29–41
Alito, Samuel, 49

B

Brown v. Board of Education of
   Topeka, 11
Bush, Jeb, 46–47

C

Civil Rights Act of 1964, 12–14, 15,
   18, 19, 23, 25, 43, 47, 55
Clinton, Bill, 37, 38, 39–40
Commission on Civil Rights, 11
Committee on Equal Employment
   Opportunity, 11–12
Connerly, Ward, 45, 46, 56,
   57–58, 61

D

Dirksen, Everett, 19
Downey, Dawn, 44

E

Eisenhower, Dwight D., 25
Equal Employment Opportunity
   Commission (EEOC), 13, 19,
   21, 22–23
executive orders, 5, 11–12, 20–21, 22

G

Gratz v. Bollinger, 49, 52
Griggs v. Duke Power Co., 25
Grutter v. Bollinger, 47–49, 52, 65

H

Hopwood v. Texas, 45–46, 58
Humphrey, Hubert, 19–20, 27
Hunter v. Erickson, 61

J

Jim Crow laws, 8, 9
Johnson, Lyndon B., 6, 12, 15, 17,
   19, 21, 22, 28
Johnson v. Santa Clara County
   Transportation Agency, 40–41

K

Kennedy, John F., 5, 11, 12, 19, 21
Klutznick, Philip M., 30

L

Lincoln, Abraham, 12

M

Meredith v. Jefferson County Board of
   Education, 50, 52

ABOUT THE AUTHOR

Mary-Lane Kamberg is a writer specializing in nonfiction for young readers. She was a junior in an all-white high school when President Lyndon B. Johnson signed the Civil Rights Act into law on July 2, 1964.

PHOTO CREDITS

Cover Mike Simons/Getty Images; p. 4 Alfred Eisenstaedt/Time & Life Pictures/Getty Images; p. 8 Paul Schutzer/Time & Life Pictures/Getty Images; pp. 10, 26 National Archives/Hulton Archive/Getty Images; p. 14 Hulton Archive/Getty Images; p. 16 LBJ Library photo by Yoichi Okamoto; p. 18 Bob Gomel/Time & Life Pictures/Getty Images; pp. 21, 24, 32–33, 34–35, 43, 50–51, 54–55, 57, 58–59, 62–63, © AP Images; p. 31 Duane Howell/The Denver Post/Getty Images; p. 39 Luke Frazza/AFP/Getty Images; p. 48 Michael L. Abramson/Time & Life Pictures/Getty Images; cover and interior background images © iStockphoto.com/Victor Pelaez (U. S. Constitution facsimile), © iStockphoto.com/klikk (American flag).

Designer: Nicole Russo; Editor: Jeanne Nagle;
Photo Researcher: Karen Huang